FROM ZERO

HARNESSING DARK EMOTIONS TO BUILD WEALTH AND SUCCESS

UNDERDOG

From Zero: Harnessing Dark Emotions to Build Wealth and Success

Copyright © 2024 by Underdog

All rights reserved.

ISBN: 979-8-329-05639-6

First Edition

Printed in the United States of America

No part of this book may be reproduced in any form or by any electronic or mechanical means, including information storage and retrieval systems, without written permission from the author, except for the use of brief quotations in a book review.

MY 'GROUND ZERO'

Everyone has a story.

When I was in high school, my father's business went bankrupt. It was a few years after the 2008 subprime mortgage crisis. My father, burdened with nearly 1.5 million dollars in debt, filed for bankruptcy and began personal rehabilitation. My mother, who co-signed the loans, also ended up with a ruined credit score. Every manufacturing business around my father's workplace collapsed, leading to a series of business owners' suicides in the industrial complex. My strong-willed father seemed to lose his sanity from that point, wandering aimlessly for over a decade. Our family was under close watch by the courts, the National Tax Service, and debt collectors.

I was a high school freshman at the time, with a very young sibling. Our home was often without food. In desperation, we rented a shabby place on the third floor of a building in an entertainment district. The area was littered with karaoke bars frequented by call girls, PC rooms, and pubs. The summers were unbearably hot, and every day we encountered cockroaches. Winters were freezing, and sometimes the pipes would burst, forcing me to wash my hair at the high school sinks. Bus fare for my commute was hard to come by, so I walked an hour to school and an hour back.

When poverty enters the front door, love exits through the window. I woke up every morning to the brutal sounds of my parents fighting. Our home was a wreck of nicotine, alcohol, and violence. I once tried to defend my mother from my father's beatings, only to get beaten myself. I would go to school with bruises, and most teachers treated me like an outcast. What could I possibly say at school?

That was my starting point.

CONTENTS

Prologue   1

PART I

1. Loneliness – 'The Dark Knight'   7
2. Jealousy – 'Amadeus'   11
3. Anger - Django Unchained   14
4. Pain - John Wick 4   18
5. Depression - Fury   21

PART II

6. Reason - On the Most Rational Response   27
7. The Destination is Set   30
8. Labor - Preemptive Strikes   33
9. Investing – It's a Must   36
10. Business – A Choice   52
11. Reading, Exercise, Relationships   56

Epilogue   61

Had I the heavens' embroidered cloths,
Enwrought with golden and silver light,
The blue and the dim and the dark cloths
Of night and light and the half light,
I would spread the cloths under your feet:
But I, being poor, have only my dreams;
I have spread my dreams under your feet;
Tread softly because you tread on my dreams.

'He wishes for the Cloths of Heaven' – William Butler Yeats (1865-1939)

PROLOGUE

Are you struggling? Feeling exhausted? Want to rest? Afraid of people? Can't sleep at night? Don't feel like seeing anyone? Relying on antidepressants and sleeping pills? Can't see a future? Craving alcohol? Longing for a relationship? Finding no meaning in anything? Feeling like you're being sucked into a drain of depression? Completely abandoned your pure desire for hope?

The following text will delve into and explore our dark and complex inner selves. Like Japanese sushi chefs meticulously dissecting a large tuna, we'll use words instead of knives to lay bare each part for examination. Why do this?

We live in an era of comparison and jealousy, burdened by internal conflicts. As a result, some people drink excessively, harming their livers, while others smoke heavily, damaging their lungs. Some fixate on romantic pursuits, and others indulge in nightlife and luxury items, hastening their own ruin. They all carry self-destructive karma.

Perspectivism means everyone sees the same thing differently, making it impossible to grasp its true form. For example, some see a red lipstick as red, others as crimson, others as scarlet. The conclusion is that it's impossible to persuade others since everyone perceives things differently.

However, there are tools to overcome perspectivism: numbers, data, facts, and truth. When you say the number 1, everyone understands there is one of something. A 70% probability means 7 out of 10 samples work. When the news reports, "Several people died due to a specific cause," it's taken at face value. Statements like "Everyone dies" are undeniable truths. These do not need persuasion.

To move from self-destruction to a positive direction, we need to embrace fundamental change. We must understand this peacefully, without resistance. Even if the world's wisest sage says something is right or wrong, humans tend to stick to their beliefs due to perspectivism. Such stubbornness hinders change.

Our goal is to dissect our nature in a data-driven way. By doing so, we can handle it from the perspectives of numbers, probabilities, facts, and truths. This transforms it into a tool to overcome perspectivism, allowing for acceptance without internal resistance. This is the most natural and certain way to fundamentally change people.

Now, let's dive in. We'll categorize and explore prominent negative emotions in humans. To make the reading smooth, we'll bring in popular movies, extracting philosophical insights from synopses and characters, as if brewing coffee. This will elevate our understanding of these negative emotions. The higher the understanding, the broader the view. Just like how beings in the third dimension can omnipotently manipulate the second dimension of lines and points.

We're brainwashed to believe negative emotions are entirely bad. According to studies from Georgetown and Harvard, negative emotions are about seven times more powerful than positive ones. If so, wouldn't intentionally distorting that powerful force for constructive plans make it seven times more efficient? The key is setting the right direction to avoid misuse. This is the precise meaning of elevating the level of understanding.

After raising this level, we'll utilize reason to enact change. We'll outline plans for living a virtuous, strong life, based on the world's numbers, probabilities, facts, and truths. Such rational plans apply to anyone, regardless of their circumstances.

Even if you wonder where it all went wrong.

Even a worm wriggles when stepped on, and if we were born human with a 1 in 400 trillion chance, we must at least fight valiantly. No matter how tough the times are, simply giving in is a waste of life. I will pour all my life force into concluding this writing. I hope this book becomes a practical tool for young people worn out by life.

PART I

1

LONELINESS – 'THE DARK KNIGHT'

One of the memorable Batman movies, 'The Dark Knight,' features Heath Ledger's outstanding performance as the Joker. Let's discuss the final scene. In Gotham City, District Attorney Harvey Dent, a symbol of justice and hope, loses his girlfriend Rachel because of the Joker. Manipulated by the Joker, Dent believes the police and Batman caused her death. He takes Commissioner Gordon's son hostage to threaten Batman. To save the boy, Batman pushes Dent, causing him to fall to his death. The Commissioner despairs over the fall of Gotham's White Knight.

Batman says, "We can't let the Joker win." He then takes the blame for everything, urging the police and media to chase him as a criminal. The movie ends with Batman fleeing and the police in pursuit, hence the title 'The Dark Knight,' the 'silent guardian.'

Stoic philosophy underpins this. Its foundational text is Marcus Aurelius' 'Meditations.' As the last of Rome's Five Good Emperors, he spent his life on the battlefield. 'Meditations' is like a Roman version of Admiral Yi's war diary. Though he was naturally suited to be a scholar, constant invasions forced him to fight at the borders his entire life. He died in a modest field camp, a testament to his responsibility.

Stoic philosophy ponders when humans can find true peace. From our current point, an eternity lies in the past and future. Regardless of wealth, poverty, power, or status, all we have is the fleeting present. If we don't find peace in the present, we never will. To find inner peace, one must always strive to do morally right things, such as practicing virtue within one's community.

Therefore, Stoic philosophy is indifferent to things like death, illness, pain, poverty, loneliness, and misfortune, which ordinary people deem bad. It neither fears nor desires wealth, power, comfort, happiness, or health. It remains indifferent. The only thing a Stoic fears is becoming an incomplete human. Conversely, they aspire to maintain a state of philosophical completeness, known as 'apatheia.'

Practically, our community is our family and, extending further, close friends. Living a virtuous life in one's community, based on Stoic philosophy, inherently involves sacrifice. This is because for others to be comfortable, one must endure hardship. This sacrifice brings intense loneliness.

Let me illustrate this vividly. If your parents work hard every day despite their old age, while you travel, buy luxury goods, and enjoy a carefree life, can you truly say you're living a happy life? Men, women, and entertainment can temporarily distract from loneliness and pain. But no normal person can feel inner peace with such a lifestyle. It weighs on their conscience because their parents are their parents, and their siblings are their siblings.

Conversely, living a life based on Stoic principles brings inevitable pain and loneliness, but the soul remains at peace. The substance created through my pain and loneliness will enrich my parents' and siblings' lives. When this is fully realized, we can deeply recognize that we have practiced virtue in our community. True peace will then settle in our souls.

We could die in two minutes, two hours, two weeks, two months, or two years. Who can guarantee our survival? If you were to die immediately, what kind of life would you need to live to have no regrets? It's not a difficult problem. Becoming a 'Dark Knight,' a 'silent guardian' indifferent to pain and loneliness, is a noble, honorable, and peaceful way to live.

Ji-sung Park

With an average of 3 successful tackles per 90 minutes, a tackle success rate of 73%, 2 interceptions, 4 recoveries, and a ground duel success rate of nearly 54%, Ji-sung Park was renowned for his defensive prowess, specializing in neutralizing key players (he once defeated AC Milan legend Andrea Pirlo).

He exhibited an exceptional work rate, covering 6-7.5 miles per match, applying relentless forward pressure. Whenever an opposing player turned their back, slowed down, lost the ball, or held onto it for too long, Park would immediately press hard.

Manchester United fans nicknamed him 'Three Lung Park' due to his seemingly boundless stamina.

Ji-sung Park retired due to a knee injury that caused recurring fluid buildup.

During Cristiano Ronaldo's peak from 2006-2008, Park was always deployed in midfield. Manager Alex Ferguson believed only Park could support Ronaldo's balance. After Ronaldo moved to another club, Park's match appearances decreased.

Alex Ferguson called Ji-sung Park Manchester United's 'most underrated player.'

2

JEALOUSY – 'AMADEUS'

Amadeus is a film about the genius composer Mozart and his envious rival, Salieri. Although inspired by historical events, it takes creative liberties. The film centers on Salieri's jealousy. Despite his own considerable talent, Salieri couldn't match Mozart's brilliance. Driven by this, Salieri plots to destroy Mozart, causing him to lose his reputation and sanity, ultimately leading to his death. Despite this, Salieri continues to admire Mozart's masterpieces, showing a dual nature of admiration and envy. This 1984 film won the Academy Award for Best Picture.

What struck me most about this film was its self-deprecating tone. Self-deprecation means 'mocking oneself.' Through 'Amadeus,' the director conveyed that humans are inherently creatures of jealousy. It seemed like an inherent part of human nature.

Teachings from Buddhism, ancient Jewish wisdom, the Quran, and other sources usually condemn jealousy, deeming it unwise and immoral. Yet, we all experience jealousy. We often recognize it in ourselves when we envy others.

We live in the stark reality of Korea. East Asian culture places a strong emphasis on others' perceptions. Moreover, media and social media now fill our time constantly. Unlike the Middle East or America, Korea lacks a pervasive religious belief system, leading to a value system largely based on material wealth. Consequently, Korea has the highest consumption of luxury goods in the world. Extreme jealousy over money sometimes leads to violence. News reports cases where spouses harm each other for life insurance payouts.

I mention this not to judge these situations but to state the facts. Basing our discussion on facts allows us to engage our reason, and reason must be engaged for actions to work in reality.

The choice is simple: live by human instinct and embrace jealousy, or try to suppress jealousy against our natural tendencies. Most self-help books advocate for suppressing jealousy, but I think differently. Jealousy is a form of energy. If we can harness this potent energy, which comes effortlessly, for productive activities, wouldn't it be beneficial?

The issue is direction. Without proper direction, this energy can lead to self-destructive behaviors, comparing oneself to those better off. However, if we channel this energy towards achieving similar success, we create an endless supply of motivation. Thus, there's no need to suppress it. It's a highly efficient, eco-friendly energy source.

John F. Kennedy (35th President of the United States)

On April 12, 1961, Soviet cosmonaut Yuri Gagarin became the first human to journey into outer space.

The Soviet Union claimed the titles of the first successful satellite launch, the first living creature in space, and the first human spaceflight. This instilled a sense of security threat in the US, fearing Soviet nuclear capabilities reaching their homeland.

Contrary to America's previous passive stance on space exploration, Kennedy aggressively pushed for space development to surpass the Soviets in space exploration and ballistic missile capabilities. His goal was a manned lunar landing, declaring:

> "We choose to go to the moon in this decade [...], not because they are easy, but because they are hard, because that goal will serve to organize and measure the best of our energies and skills, because that challenge is one that we are willing to accept, one we are unwilling to postpone, and one which we intend to win."

On July 20, 1969, Apollo 11's lunar module, the Eagle, landed, and Neil Armstrong took the first step on the moon.

3

ANGER - DJANGO UNCHAINED

Django Unchained by Quentin Tarantino is my all-time favorite movie. The film follows Django, a former black slave, who, with the help of his ally Dr. Schultz, becomes a free man and sets out to rescue his wife from a cruel plantation owner. Django and Dr. Schultz devise a plan to free Django's wife from a large cotton plantation called "Candyland," owned by Calvin Candy. To conceal their true intentions, they pretend to be interested in purchasing a Mandingo fighter, a brutal form of entertainment involving slave fights popular at the time.

Schultz offers to buy one of Candy's Mandingo fighters for an outrageously high price, using this as a pretext to also purchase Django's wife, who happens to speak German - a rare trait for a black slave. During dinner negotiations, Django's wife serves the white guests, while an elderly black head slave serves Candy. Sensing something between Django and his wife, the head slave informs Candy that the pair are not interested in the Mandingo fighter but intend to take the woman away.

Furious, Candy orders his men to hold Django and Dr. Schultz at gunpoint, forcing them to buy Django's wife for an exorbitant price. Despite losing a significant amount of money, Dr. Schultz waits for the contract to be finalized, intending to take Django's wife without bloodshed. However, an intense exchange ensues once the contract is signed.

As Dr. Schultz prepares to leave, he makes it clear he has no intention of seeing Candy again and turns to exit. Candy, insisting on a Southern tradition, demands a handshake to finalize their deal. Dr. Schultz refuses, expressing his disdain and trying to leave. Candy then threatens to kill Django's wife if Schultz doesn't comply, escalating the situation. Unable to tolerate Candy's arrogance and threats, Schultz shoots Candy in the heart instead of shaking hands, leading to a violent confrontation where Schultz sacrifices himself, showing that his principles and anger over injustice override his instinct for self-preservation.

When a person truly pursues a value passionately, they sometimes prioritize it over their own life. Anger, therefore, is an unmatched source of energy. Respect and admiration often follow someone willing to risk their life for a cause. This demonstrates the tremendous power of anger.

Many people say you shouldn't get angry, but I disagree. I believe anger is something you must know how to harness. When fundamental human rights are violated, one must be able to get angry. Anger serves as the most realistic fuel for recognizing, confronting, and initiating action against problems.

When people are angry, they are designed to act. New nations and civilizations have often been birthed by the anger of a few. Think of the Korean independence movement during Japanese rule or the Boston Tea Party that sparked American independence.

Anger also helps to break free from other negative emotions that hamper productivity, such as depression, loneliness, and pain. When adrenaline is released and the heart rate increases, those feelings disappear, leaving only boundless energy like a volcano.

However, anger is a double-edged sword that must be used carefully. Unleashing raw anger can harm oneself and others due to its potent energy. It should be controlled and used deliberately, much like harnessing nuclear energy for power rather than letting it explode. To use anger strategically, channel it into productive actions. You could do countless push-ups, run over 6 miles, or, like me, write intensely. If you're in business, ramp up your marketing and promotion. Increase your savings and investment efforts. Make a detailed career, asset, and skill manifest on a large whiteboard and devise the most efficient battle strategy.

Django, a former black slave, overcame numerous adversities and ultimately became a free man, rescuing his wife and achieving a happy ending. What made this possible was the boundless energy of his anger, not merely motivation or willpower.

Bang Si-hyuk (CEO of Big Hit Entertainment - home to BTS) spoke at a Seoul National University graduation.

"I pondered deeply about the source of the energy that made me who I am today. It was none other than 'anger.'"

"Reflecting on my journey, the image that clearly stands out is 'angry Bang Si-hyuk.' I was furious with mediocrity and complacency, driven by a mission to create the best content without compromise, living each day as if it were my last."

"**The music industry's situation was irrational, and I was angry about it.** I will continue to fight so that music industry workers receive fair evaluation and proper treatment."

"Graduates will encounter much irrationality and absurdity in their journey ahead. I hope you get angry and fight against injustice to change society."

4

PAIN - JOHN WICK 4

John Wick 4 is the fourth installment in the John Wick series and a significant part of Keanu Reeves' filmography. While the series is known for its stunning action sequences, it also has a deep philosophical undertone.

Let's talk about the staircase scene set in Paris. John Wick, with a bounty on his head, is being hunted by every assassin. To win his freedom, he must climb a long set of stairs to reach the final duel.

Enemies swarm him as he ascends. Armed with only a handgun, he fights his way up, repeatedly kicked and punched, causing him to tumble down the stairs multiple times. Despite these setbacks, he never gives up and eventually reaches the duel location just in time.

This scene is filled with immense time pressure, significant stress, and extreme physical and mental pain. Yet, John Wick perseveres. What drove him? It wasn't just sheer willpower; it was a high threshold.

All living beings, including humans, have a threshold—the minimum level of stimulus required to trigger a reaction. When we consume very sweet food, less sweet food seems tasteless because our threshold has increased. Thus, a higher stimulus is needed to feel the same level of sweetness. The threshold can be raised but not lowered.

Patrick Henry, a leader of the American Revolution, is famous for his speech declaring, "Give me liberty, or give me death."

One of the most powerful and profound stimuli a human can experience is freedom. This assertion isn't based on some cheerful, textbook notion. Rather, it's because the financial cost of maintaining freedom is incredibly high. To live without ever having to ask for favors and to speak your mind whenever and wherever you want is invaluable. If you can't freely express yourself without risking your livelihood, such as losing your job, you aren't truly free. Therefore, someone who can avoid such constraints and live a fulfilling life is considered free. This makes freedom the most expensive commodity. Unlike cars, houses, or luxury goods, which you buy once and then own, freedom must be sustained over decades. When you add up all the costs of maintaining freedom, it becomes the most valuable stimulus.

When someone experiences a breakthrough in freedom, lesser stimuli no longer register with them. As a result, they lose the motivation to pursue these lesser stimuli. There are countless values in the world, but none match the intensity of freedom. Thus, a person who realizes this will devote all their resources—physical, mental, material, and temporal—to achieving freedom.

John Wick sought freedom from the pressures of the High Table and the bounty on his head. He endured the pain honestly and persistently. Other material possessions held no interest for him because his threshold system was geared toward achieving freedom.

In summary, what people often refer to as willpower doesn't have enough energy to overcome pain. If it did, we'd see many more people overcoming pain through willpower alone.

Therefore, the energy to overcome pain comes only from a high threshold level.

Elon Musk faced backlash for supporting conspiracy theories on Twitter. During an interview on this topic, the host questioned why Musk would make such statements online, potentially harming Tesla or Twitter's sales.

> Elon Musk: "There's a scene in a movie where a character confronts the person who killed his father and says, 'Offer me money. Offer me power. I don't care.'"
>
> Host: "So you just don't care. You want to share what you have to say?"
>
> Elon Musk: "I'll say what I want to say, and if the consequence of that is losing money, so be it."

5

DEPRESSION - FURY

Fury is a World War II movie that tells the story of an American tank crew advancing against German forces. The crew, nicknamed "Fury," highlights the harsh realities of war and the psychological toll it takes on soldiers.

The film shows soldiers facing the primal fear of death amid fierce battles. After surviving these battles, they momentarily relax with a cigarette, relieved to be alive. When they return to the base and a sense of safety is somewhat assured, they struggle with severe depression. The tank commander, aware of this, keeps his crew busy even during downtime, ordering them to clean, replenish water, food, and ammunition. I found this scene particularly impactful.

Depression brings no benefits. It lacks energy and, in fact, drains it. It can even cause physical harm to the brain and body. Prolonged exposure to cortisol can slow the creation of new neurons in the hippocampus and reduce the volume of brain cells, leading to memory decline. Therefore, depression is not a resource to be utilized but an enemy to be repelled, blocked, and suppressed.

As humans with intellectual capabilities, we need to be engaged in something to avoid going mad. Feeling bored and restless is a sign of this. That's why most people seek out fun activities. However, life has a threshold, and pursuing endless short-term pleasures only leads to a continuous increase in the threshold for pleasure, which can result in self-destruction. The ultimate extreme of seeking pleasure is drug addiction, with alcohol, travel, luxury, sexual satisfaction, and gambling often leading the way.

Therefore, seeking fun is just a quick fix for depression, not a proper defense or suppression. The true way to fend off depression is to immerse yourself in a grand project - something challenging, painful, and long-term. This could be asset-building, achieving religious enlightenment, endless pursuit in arts, philosophy, and science, or pushing physical limits through triathlons and ultramarathons. As shown in the movie Fury, the best way to fend off depression is to continually engage yourself in purposeful tasks.

Winston Churchill (61st and 63rd Prime Minister of the United Kingdom)

Churchill struggled with severe depression. **To cope, he took up painting and writing (he even won the Nobel Prize in Literature).** He once said he wished to paint for eternity in heaven. These activities helped alleviate but never fully cured his depression. He avoided balconies and train tracks to prevent impulsive suicide attempts.

Churchill is one of the most renowned British Prime Ministers, leading Britain through WWII with fierce resistance against Nazi Germany, ultimately turning the tide for the Allies.

> "We shall go on to the end, we shall fight in France, we shall fight on the seas and oceans, we shall fight with growing confidence and growing strength in the air, we shall defend our Island, whatever the cost may be, we shall fight on the beaches, we shall fight on the landing grounds, we shall fight in the fields and in the streets, we shall fight in the hills; we shall never surrender."
>
> – June 4, 1940, House of Commons speech

PART II

6

REASON - ON THE MOST RATIONAL RESPONSE

Once you've mastered harnessing negative emotions as outlined earlier, you will be reborn as a powerful warrior capable of immense energy. You'll become an indomitable force. Over ten or twenty years, your life will undergo a profound transformation.

Living in South Korea today, we must decide what to pursue by manipulating and utilizing various negative emotions. Everyone has their own principles, but I want to focus on the most honest direction.

In South Korea, traditional national ideologies like Confucianism have largely faded. We don't really have a state religion either. The only value system most citizens acknowledge is economic power. Whether this is right or wrong is beside the point; it's a fact that everyone must accept.

While I'm discussing South Korea, this scenario applies to many other countries, including the United States and other parts of the modern world. Traditional ideologies and religious influences have diminished globally, with economic power becoming the dominant value system. People everywhere must recognize and adapt to this reality.

Thus, from the most honest standpoint, the surest tool to practice virtues for the community and achieve peace of mind is money. This becomes the dominant factor, leading everyone to become obsessed with money. I believe those striving to enhance their economic power are doing the right thing because they are confronting the reality of their circumstances. It's a very logical approach.

Living without any regrets or excuses involves a lifestyle focused solely on this goal. It means no lingering desires or excuses for the usual pleasures people seek, such as work-life balance, romance, travel, shopping, cars, or homes. Their primary objective is to take good care of their community and family.

Having organized the facts about human negative emotions, we will now discuss the theories and battle strategies needed in practice.

In my twenties, I tried various jobs: full-time, contract, day labor, entrepreneurship, stock investment, real estate auctions, publishing, and social media activities. While I couldn't excel at everything, I eventually found significant success in stock investment after many failures. I'll share insights from the last ten years of data, which should be quite relevant.

Before diving in, I want to emphasize that this is akin to building a vast independent empire.

Empires aren't built overnight.

They require sacrifices and pain. If you start from nothing, against your will, sacrifices and pain may mean losing your youth, damaging your health, and even risking your life.

If you have a clear purpose, prepare yourself mentally and take it seriously.

7

THE DESTINATION IS SET

Long ago, there was a scholar who compiled comprehensive knowledge about the goals we should strive to achieve. His name was Thorstein Veblen, the author of "The Theory of the Leisure Class." In English, the term "leisure class" describes a group of individuals engaged in fields like politics, warfare, sports, investment, art, and religion. The common thread among these professions is their detachment from actual productive activities.

These professions all originated from early human societies where hunting was a prestigious occupation. In prehistoric times, hunters and warriors were considered honorable, while other tasks such as maintenance, cooking, transportation, household chores, making clothes and jewelry, and processing animal carcasses were deemed lowly. Simply by being involved in a field not directly related to production, these professionals subtly indicated their belonging to the leisure class. Consequently, they naturally held a certain level of honor within their community.

Today's leisure class is distinguished by the amount of their assets, the most definitive metric. Even professionals aren't necessarily part of this leisure class. For example, many doctors are salaried, and lawyers aren't entirely free from business constraints. As of 2024 in Korea, having a net cash asset of at least $800,000 is the threshold for the leisure class. This threshold generally marks the point where individuals can live comfortably without needing to work, as they can generate enough cash flow from their assets, which, when reinvested, continue to grow over time. However, it's important to note that this benchmark will increase over time due to inflation.

One cliché that I find particularly misleading is the saying, "Success should come slowly." I believe this notion is fundamentally flawed. Inflation erodes our assets constantly—whether we're eating, sleeping, or going about our daily activities. Since wages typically increase more slowly than inflation, the slower we accumulate assets, the more disadvantaged we become. Moreover, the time we have to benefit from compound interest diminishes every moment we delay.

There's a concept called "entropy" and the "second law of thermodynamics." Entropy measures the degree of disorder in a system. Higher entropy means more disorder, and lower entropy means less disorder. The second law of thermodynamics states that the total entropy of an isolated system always increases or remains constant over time. Humans are part of nature, so the second law applies to human affairs, including money. Left to human instincts, our spending entropy increases over time, leading to financial disorder.

The bottom line is that over time, it becomes harder to organize our finances and live properly. The earlier we impose control, the easier it is.

Missing out on speed and momentum can lead to dire consequences, so be acutely aware of this. This concerns your own benefit; failing to recognize it only harms you. There are natural laws beyond our control.

To sum up, our ultimate destination and new starting point is having $800,000 in cash assets, and achieving this requires rapid momentum.

8

LABOR - PREEMPTIVE STRIKES

As of 2024, the average median disposable income of the working population in South Korea is around $1,700 per month. Most people earn this by working 5-7 days a week. I present this figure to set realistic expectations. The pervasive influence of social media and success fantasies has distorted many people's perspectives on money. This is a major trap that can prevent individuals from reaching financial stability.

We must base our decisions solely on numbers, statistics, probabilities, and facts. These provide the most reliable foundation in reality. Claims of easily earning millions or billions should be viewed skeptically. All money, no matter how small, is valuable and should be treated with care.

If your family cannot comfortably support you through 4-6 years of private university while securing their own retirement, it is crucial to start working as soon as possible. Most people likely fall outside this category. It's crucial to get money into your account as quickly as possible. The reason? To enjoy the benefits of compound interest as early as you can. While I gently suggest avoiding university, the data clearly shows that not attending is often the better choice.

You need to strike a deal with your parents. Propose to take half of what they would spend on college tuition upfront, and in return, you'll forgo college. Instead, start preparing for a civil service exam in high school, or if studying isn't your thing, dive into an entry-level job in a field that interests you. The lump sum you get upfront should be immediately invested to earn returns that outpace inflation each year. This way, your parents save 50% on college expenses, and you secure your seed money quickly. It's a win-win for both parties.

Our bodies will inevitably deteriorate, despite our best efforts. The physical peak occurs in the late teens to mid-twenties, a period of Wolverine-like recovery. The younger you are, the more you should push yourself to earn as much money as possible. This is a logical strategy. Bet on compound interest by pouring your time and effort into earning as much money as possible early on.

Remember, the money you get your hands on at this stage of life is more powerful than any other money you'll earn later on. For example, if we assume an average annual return rate of 25%, $100,000 today could grow to $1 million in 10 years, $10 million in 20 years, and $100 million in 30 years.

Put as much effort into saving money as you do into earning it. Every dollar is worth it. Living rent-free with your parents is fantastic if you can. If that's not an option, consider splitting the rent with a sibling or a close friend. Another option is to move into a dorm-like living arrangement. Besides buying food and essentials to survive, avoid any other expenses. Every penny saved should go straight into your investment account.

This will be the toughest and most brutal period. If you endure this time of intense sacrifice better than anyone else, you're halfway there. This period is critical and impactful. Think of it as a war.

Even past your mid-twenties, continue earning labor income until you reach financial stability. To understand the economic value of earning $1,700 a month, consider the equivalent asset value. Assuming a 2% bank interest rate, having $1 million in a savings account would be needed to withdraw $1,700 monthly. Thus, earning $1,700 monthly is equivalent to holding $1 million in the bank.

9

INVESTING – IT'S A MUST

Investing is not optional; it's essential. Inflation is relentlessly catching up. Ignoring this simple fact can lead to disaster. Numbers don't lie. People lie and turn a blind eye.

There's a lot of talk about investing, but based on my personal experience over the past decade, the most effective ways to grow wealth are through stocks or real estate. Other forms of investment either don't offer much return for the time and energy spent or are dangerously close to gambling. So, you just need to choose between these two.

Before deciding on a big category, you need to understand yourself, especially how much risk you can handle. If, like me, you started life with nothing or even with debt, it's natural to take on as much risk as possible. However, everyone's maximum risk tolerance is different. This isn't something learned but something inherent. Compare yourself to those around you to gauge your limits.

There are broadly two types of investors: the "Warren Buffett type" and the "Elon Musk type."

The "Warren Buffett type" doesn't use debt. They prefer common-sense moves. They compare data and figures, betting on the simplest and most obvious things, and they know how to wait patiently. Berkshire Hathaway is famous for holding onto stocks for a long time once they're purchased.

The "Elon Musk type" uses debt. They prefer a more instinctive approach. While they check the basics, they seek extreme, rapid momentum, often overriding conventional wisdom. If things go well, their assets grow quickly; if not, they take significant hits. Even when Elon Musk faces severe setbacks, he overcomes them with superhuman tenacity, using any means necessary.

If you're a "Warren Buffett type," stocks are for you. If you're an "Elon Musk type," real estate is better. Stocks allow investment without debt, while real estate typically requires debt. Neither is inherently better; you should decide based on your style.

I'm a "Warren Buffett type," so I've been investing in securities for the past decade, achieving around a 20% annual return. Let's review the steps to improve your investing skills, which include both technical and philosophical skills, both essential for making money.

On Technical Skills

If you're new to investing and have little interest in economics, you usually start by looking at your local market. If you have any interest in economics, you look at the US market. This is a straightforward, very logical decision. Would you bet on the team captain or the benchwarmer? Some avoid the US market due to capital gains tax, but taxes are only for those who make money, not those who lose it. These people often stay in their local market and don't talk about stocks after a series of losses. Common sense is key. The world has its order, and ignoring it brings consequences. Stocks are part of this worldly order.

The first thing to try from scratch is index tracking. I'll explain why in the section on philosophical skills.

There are various indexes, but you should follow the one that tracks the NASDAQ because it includes the world's biggest companies. ETFs that track the NASDAQ are available, and you should keep buying one of these. The main ETF is SPY (ticker). With an annual average return of 7-12%, it can beat inflation. Since all you need to do is keep buying, it doesn't require much skill. Here are some more options:

- **QQQ:** Tracks the top 100 NASDAQ tech stocks.
- **SPY, VOO, IVV, SPLG:** Tracks the top 500 US companies (S&P 500).
- **DIA:** Tracks 30 major US companies listed on the stock exchange.

Expected Returns:

- **QQQ:** About 13% annually.
- **SPY:** About 10% annually.
- **SPLG:** About 13% annually.
- **DIA:** About 10% annually.

Dividend yields and management fees differ, so pick one that suits you best. You must protect your investment account like it's your life unless it's for something major like a funeral or a severe illness. Even in war, you should protect this account. Otherwise, it loses its meaning.

Some recommend funds made by insurance or financial companies. I disagree, based on personal experience.

Financial products are not covered by FDIC insurance (individual stocks are recorded by the depository and can be recovered even if the brokerage fails, and amounts up to $250,000 are covered by FDIC insurance). Additionally, these products often come with significant fees that can greatly reduce returns. This only applies when there's profit. Many funds actually record losses, and fees are still charged regardless.

When you invest in a fund, you get reports. Few people actually read them carefully, but I did. There's a turnover ratio, which shows how much the fund buys and sells stocks. The higher the turnover, the better the internal performance of the fund manager, but this means more transaction fees are deducted. So, it's good for the fund company employees but bad for the actual owners of the money. The turnover ratio is not transparently shown in reports. I once grilled my financial consultant about this but got no clear answers. They hush it up. Is this what you want? You need to get your money back.

If you're born with limited resources, you need to learn the strategies available in the market. There's no other way to build wealth. I was in the same position. I didn't know anything about stocks at first, and I spent countless hours combing through bookstores. Here, I introduce the strategies I learned from the books I found useful.

Quant Investing

The term "quant" comes from "quantitative," meaning numerical or measurable. So, quant investing refers to strategies based on statistics and mathematics. Seeing is believing, so let's look at an example.

Included Assets:

- US assets (SPY)
- Developed market stocks (EFA)
- US bonds (AGG)

Buying Strategy:

- At the end of each month, calculate the recent 12-month returns for US stocks (SPY), developed market stocks (EFA), and short-term bonds (BIL).
- If SPY's return is higher than BIL's (SPY>BIL), invest in SPY or EFA, whichever has the higher 12-month return.
- If SPY's return is lower than BIL's (SPY<BIL), invest in AGG.
- Rebalance once a month.

In this way, there is always a specific reason for a trade. The return rate is the standard for trading, making it quantitative. This style of investing is called quantitative investing. This is just one of many quant strategies, and there are various types, expected returns, capital scales, and applicable strategies.

I introduced quant investing first because it's a suitable strategy for beginners aside from index tracking. Depending on the strategy, you can choose an aggressive or defensive approach. Many hesitate due to fear of direct investment, but this provides a portfolio to overcome that fear. It involves not just stocks but bonds and gold too.

Books (Korean) by Kang Hwan-guk explain these quant strategies well. Refer to these books, decide on a strategy, and try it out.

Investing with a Less Than 3% Strategy

Although this strategy is a form of quantitative investing, it stands out due to its lack of diversification. It's not about ETFs; it focuses all funds on one or two individual stocks. Therefore, it's advisable to gain experience with more stable strategies and learn to endure losses before diving in.

To employ this strategy, you'll need to understand limit orders, automated overseas stock orders, and margin functionalities. Mastering these basic mobile trading skills is essential. Because this strategy involves concentrated investment, the target return is higher compared to general quantitative investing. Naturally, this means the speed at which your assets decrease if stock prices fall will also be faster.

This strategy relies on specific trading criteria. The primary trigger is whether the Nasdaq index drops by 3%. Additionally, it considers factors like an eight - day consecutive rise, percentage drop from the previous high, and percentage drop from a reference price to carry out rebalancing. There's also a concept called "staking" where you accumulate shares in proportion at low points.

For detailed information, read the book (Korean) by Jordan Kim Jang-seop. He runs a forum called 'JD Wealth Research Center' on Daum Cafe, where you can gain more insights. If you need further guidance, consider purchasing the author's lectures (Korean) or YouTube premium content.

VR Strategy

'VR' stands for Value Rebalancing, utilizing TQQQ. TQQQ is a leveraged ETF that tracks QQQ at three times its performance. The strategy introduces a constant termed as the 'V-value,' which is a calculated figure tracking TQQQ's price. Concepts of maximum and minimum thresholds are also introduced, recalculated based on the 'V-value.'

A graph is plotted using the 'V-value,' and maximum and minimum thresholds are drawn over it. When the 'V-value' touches the maximum threshold, you sell. When it touches the minimum threshold, you buy.

This strategy is highly volatile and aims for substantial returns. It's the highest risk and reward strategy among those presented and is not recommended for beginners. In a major crisis like the dot-com bubble or subprime mortgage crisis, this strategy could fail completely.

For more details, read 'Value Rebalancing of U.S. Stocks' by Raoo. This strategy is highly volatile and aims for substantial returns. It's the highest risk and reward strategy among those presented and is not recommended for beginners. The author admits that in a major crisis like the dot-com bubble or subprime mortgage crisis, this strategy could fail completely.

The book's subtitle is 'You Can't Change an Ordinary Life Without Leverage.' That should give you a sense of the approach.

Practical Data on Stock Investing

Understanding Limit Orders

Most people start trading using a trading app. When placing trades, you have several options, with limit orders being the default. A limit order ensures the trade is executed at the best possible price near the specified price. It may take some time for the order to be filled. Some people get impatient and keep placing new orders, which is unnecessary and self-defeating. Practice patience by leaving your order and doing something else, ensuring it's executed at your desired price.

Fees and Reliability

Major brokers typically include firms like Merrill Lynch, Charles Schwab, and J.P. Morgan. Others like Vanguard, Fidelity, and Goldman Sachs are also reliable. It's generally best to choose a major broker, but there's no need to worry much about fees and stability among these large firms. Wasting time being indecisive can be a bigger loss.

However, avoid smaller brokers due to their size. They can be risky in volatile times. Personally, I'd also avoid certain firms due to negative rumors and a dubious reputation.

Taxes on Foreign Stock Investments

When you profit from foreign stocks, your capital gains tax is calculated on the profit, which is the difference between your selling price and the purchase cost (cost basis). These gains are subject to federal tax and, depending on your state, may also be subject to state taxes. Most brokers offer free tools to help calculate these capital gains.

Keep in mind, the effect of currency exchange rates can significantly impact your calculated gains or losses. For example, if you bought stocks in a foreign currency that has since appreciated against the dollar, you may face a higher tax bill, as your gains in dollar terms will appear larger. Conversely, if the foreign currency has depreciated, your taxable gain may be less, or you might even realize a loss.

A common misconception surrounds the wash sale rule. If you sell stocks at a loss and repurchase similar stocks within a 30 - day window, the IRS will disallow the loss as a tax deduction. This rule prevents taxpayers from claiming a tax benefit while maintaining a position in the same stock or a substantially similar one. Therefore, it's usually more beneficial to manage your investments with the long-term tax implications in mind rather than attempting to exploit this rule for temporary tax relief.

Watching the Federal Reserve's Base Rate

In the U.S. market, over 90% of stock movements are influenced by the Federal Reserve's base rate trends. Thus, there's little practical benefit in trying to study and apply various indicators technically. Understanding the general direction of the current big trends is sufficient. Base rate changes are typically priced into the market about six months in advance, which can guide your investment decisions.

Perspectives on Real Estate Investment

If you're not born into a family where your parents have comfortably prepared for retirement and can effortlessly support your college tuition for four to six years, then you're likely going to face life's challenges on your own merit. More specifically, this includes families with a net worth around $50,000 or those who are even in debt. Most young people today don't fall into this category.

This is just the surface level of assets, but it hints at a broader perspective. It suggests that these parents lack a foundational understanding of capitalism. Meaning, they lack experience in buying, holding, and selling assets—leaving their children without real-world financial knowledge to inherit.

In real estate, multiple parties are involved: typically real estate agents and sellers, and yes, actual contracts. This opens up potential for fraud. Looking at my peers who have succeeded in real estate, they invariably had parental support. This support isn't just about money; it's also about accompanying them to their first property deal, imparting essential knowledge and savvy to navigate the process. Having a shrewd adult in the mix usually makes it harder for brokers or sellers to play games. These parents possess a high level of knowledge, capable of sniffing out dubious terms in agreements.

However, for folks like me, born into outright poverty, we lack this support.

You can work yourself to the bone to save up seed money. I've watched many hustle hard, visiting multiple real estate offices, which I believe is quite risky. To brokers and sellers, someone like this is easy prey—full of money and passion but lacking in knowledge and backup.

When you think about real estate, the fact that most transactions involve borrowing makes it inherently risky. Legendary investor Peter Lynch, who managed the renowned Magellan Fund at Fidelity, highlighted the unpredictable nature of interest rates. He argued that no one, not even the experts, can reliably predict interest rate movements. While the Fed Chair might have an idea of where short-term rates are headed in the next three to six months, predicting where they will be in three to five years is another matter entirely. This raises an important question: if even the experts at the Federal Reserve struggle with long-term forecasts, how can individual investors hope to predict these changes? This perspective is crucial for anyone involved in markets affected by interest rates, like real estate, where understanding these limitations on predictability can inform safer, more informed investment strategies.

Young people in Korea who overextended themselves in 2022 are paying dearly for it now, facing what feels like a lost decade or two. It's baffling why such a high proportion of investments in South Korea are tied up in real estate when it so often doesn't make sense.

Charlie Munger, the longtime collaborator of the late Warren Buffett, once shared some wisdom that underscores a lot of his success. He emphasized the importance of using common sense in decision-making. Munger believed that by simply doing fewer foolish things than others, he managed to achieve greater success. This approach, he suggested, played a significant role in his accomplishments.

Those favorable towards real estate investment argue it's because asset appreciation can be rapid, especially when leveraging over half the purchase price. If things go well, the gains can be swift. However, people need to be aware of the risks involved.

If you still want to invest in real estate, public auctions might be worth considering because they can potentially offer properties at lower prices. Even if you use a loan, it's generally less than what you'd need otherwise. Additionally, transactions here are overseen by the government, not middlemen. Yet, once you get into it, you realize the barriers.

I've spent time at courthouses bidding in real estate auctions. Often, the viable properties are snagged by corporate investors who can afford to bid much higher due to tax benefits. This makes it nearly impossible for individual investors to compete.

Some say to keep trying and you might get lucky. While possible, the chances of landing a good property not already targeted by corporations are slim. And even if you do win such a property, there's usually a reason why the big players stayed away—perhaps a hidden lien or other complications.

After all, real estate isn't the only asset you can invest in. Stocks, for example, are governed entirely by your own decisions and actions, making them devoid of the risk of scams. Logically, there are better and safer options available, yet the allure of real estate persists for many.

In conclusion, if you have parental support, investing in real estate might work out. If you're starting life as someone from a financially disadvantaged background, it's probably best to steer clear.

On the Importance of Investor Mindset

More important than technical prowess is investor mindset. The reasoning is clear and straightforward. It's primarily because investor mindset plays a greater role in determining whether you can make money or not. That's the bottom line.

Here's what you need for an essential investor mindset:

Common Sense Cognition that Doesn't Follow the Crowd

To make meaningful profits in stock investing, you first need to survive in the market for the long haul. Surviving means acting with common sense. For instance, heavily investing in the local market isn't sensible. The bulk of your assets should be in the U.S. market. It's also not sensible to shy away from foreign stocks due to taxes while experiencing FOMO (Fear Of Missing Out) as you watch local stocks hit their price ceilings.

Risk Tolerance

If you must build your wealth without parental help, embracing maximum risk is your only option. Investment books often hype the word 'portfolio.' They promote a hedging strategy of diversification. While this approach has stability, it unfortunately yields a mere 10% return. Those starting under tough conditions should aim for at least 20 – 30% annual returns. Based on ten years of hands-on experience, that's the highest feasible rate for most individual investors.

If your returns are 10% annually, it takes 7.2 years to double your initial capital. At 20%, it takes only 3.6 years. If you start with $100,000 aiming for $1 million, 10% would take about 23 years. At 20%, it's around 13 years. 23 years is simply too long. Hence, the insistence on remembering why you're fighting.

If you're aiming for high returns, diversification isn't the answer. You need to go all-in on one or two stocks. This means accepting the risk of putting all your eggs in one basket. Such high risk necessitates some level of stability in other aspects of your life. Despite all this, living with constant pressure and stress should become a norm, demanding robust stress resilience.

Transcendent Patience

As mentioned, gathering your initial $100,000 might take up to 20 years. But collecting that seed money is just the beginning. You need to vigorously protect your investment account and annually save a sufficient amount for capital gains taxes every year. The better you manage this, the more your wealth grows.

This journey is a long, painful war. It's a lonely march into the darkest solitude.

Thus, when it comes to stock investing, the weight of mindset far outweighs that of technique. Any retreat from the front lines of self-battle means all efforts are in vain.

I've been engaged in this battle for ten years, and the high ground is now within reach.

In the film 'The Dark Knight Rises,' a character known as Bane engages in a pivotal confrontation with Batman. During their encounter, Bane comments on the illusion and trickery often used by those unfamiliar with real power, noting that both he and Batman are beyond such tactics due to their shared past in the League of Shadows. Bane asserts his identity as a true representative of the League, intent on completing a mission started by Ra's al Ghul, and criticizes Batman's openly fierce yet flawed fighting style.

In a dramatic moment when the environment plunges into darkness due to Batman's interference, Bane taunts him, suggesting that Batman mistakenly considers darkness as an advantage, whereas Bane himself was shaped by it from birth, finding the light of day overwhelmingly bright when he finally saw it.

To truly succeed as an investor, you need a mindset like Bane's. Despite enduring tough, lonely, painful days, I remain undeterred. I don't live in fear of dying tomorrow like during my dangerous days at sea or from sudden bankruptcy as in my childhood. I'm grateful for having bus fare in my pocket, for food on the table, for warmth in the cold, and for coolness in the heat. I appreciate not living under the constant threat of falling bombs like in Eastern Europe.

I am akin to 'Bane.' Born and forged in darkness, the twenty – year journey toward becoming a wealthy investor is overwhelmingly bright compared to the grim hardships of my childhood.

Why You Should Start with Index-Following Investments

I want to address a question I previously posed about technical skills. When you embark on this journey, the first step is often gathering a substantial initial investment. At this early stage, knowledge of or mindset on investing is usually nonexistent. Therefore, it's crucial to spend time learning the theory behind the techniques and nurturing a practical investment mindset.

Since separating these stages would be too time-consuming, an efficient approach is to engage in index-tracking investments. This strategy allows you to develop both theory and mindset without the need for complex theories, while simultaneously reducing the time it takes to accumulate significant capital. It also prepares you to study direct investment strategies that can potentially yield higher returns.

As you experience your hard-earned money fluctuating with global trends over several years, you'll naturally develop a resilient mindset. As mentioned in macroeconomic discussions, major financial crises seem to occur every decade with smaller crises happening intermittently. By adhering to your strategy during these times, you'll realize that market crashes are not the end of the world.

Unless an actual apocalypse occurs, the markets will recover. And if an apocalypse were to happen, then the stock prices would be the least of your concerns—you'd be better off taking your water and emergency supplies to a bunker. Through such experiences, you will cultivate a robust investor mindset.

Once you have experienced several cycles of index-tracking investments and feel confident not to flee at market lows—and you are confident that you have mastered the advanced theories—don't hesitate to dive into direct investing.

10

BUSINESS – A CHOICE

Despite my technical expertise and investment mindset, I was never quite satisfied with my performance. I craved more momentum and faster progress. So, I ventured into personal entrepreneurship and tried my hand at online business, which taught me valuable lessons I'd like to share.

When running a business, extreme speed is crucial. You must push operations to the limit of human mental and physical capacity. Business is all about selling goods or services, and thus, marketing is essential—and it's never free. Over time, the money spent on marketing efforts accumulates, underscoring the importance of speed.

Sales must happen as quickly as possible, and therefore, any peripheral processes, even if somewhat overlooked, must be expedited to avoid a financial crunch that could ground you.

In essence, sales are vital. Even if every other aspect of the business suffers, as long as the sales are alive, the business will keep rolling. However, if sales falter, even if all else is perfect, the business can collapse overnight. In today's world, keeping sales alive and growing often means using the internet and social media; believing you can market effectively online without any costs is naive. There will always be costs, though significant personal effort can reduce them.

If you deem a business beyond redemption, don't try to revive it; shut it down quickly. Salvage whatever you can before it's completely submerged to plan for the future. Business involves a significant capital investment, large or small, and knowing when to cut losses is crucial—we aren't just doing business for the sake of it.

Losing capital meant for investment also means losing years of potential compound growth, which is a loss many times the face value. Hence, while businesses may fail, losing your capital should not be an option.

Snowfox founder Chairman Kim Seung-ho's lecture video on business principles states that 90% of businesses fail while only 10% succeed—a statistic borne from decades of successful entrepreneurship. Business is often subject to luck, and if there's only a 10% chance of success, failure must always be considered.

I started my business with the assumption it would likely fail, which is why I began with modest capital and made every effort to minimize costs.

Ultimately, I managed to generate about $20,000 a month from a single product. There was potential for growth, but catching up to competitors would have required risky moves, so I quickly shut it down. Fortunately, I was able to recover all invested capital and even made a small profit through conservative management.

Understanding U.S. Business Taxes for Small Businesses

When you register as a business owner in the U.S., you take on certain tax responsibilities, including sales tax and federal income tax. Sales tax rates and rules vary by state and are collected at the point of transaction. Federal income tax is due annually in April.

For small businesses that qualify under the Tax Cuts and Jobs Act (TCJA), there are simplified tax accounting options available if annual gross receipts are below $26 million. These options include using cash accounting methods over accrual, and not having to capitalize certain inventory costs, making tax compliance easier and less costly. It's beneficial for qualifying small businesses to start with these simplified methods and adapt as they grow and their financial needs become more complex.

Perspective on Running a Business Alongside Investments

When you manage both investments and a business, the pressure from tax obligations is substantial. In South Korea, taxes must be paid multiple times throughout the year—once in January, twice in May, and once in July. Each payment requires available funds, making it a difficult and risky endeavor. This dynamic is far from stable, often leading to a year filled with adrenaline surges. You may find yourself waking up from stress-induced nightmares or experiencing heart palpitations even in calm moments.

I have lived through these challenges, which once led to a bout of vertigo so severe I fainted. Vertigo can occur when tiny stones in the inner ear's vestibular system move out of place, causing severe dizziness, nausea, and loss of balance. I suspect extreme stress and lack of sleep were the culprits.

From this experience, I realized that my performance peaks were actually at the limit of what I could sustain. Viewing the bigger picture, I concluded that focusing entirely on investing might bring quicker gains in momentum. Thus, I argue that business involvement should be a choice. If one is truly passionate about business, it might be better to concentrate solely on one venture.

11

READING, EXERCISE, RELATIONSHIPS

Reading

When it comes to reading, I take a balanced stance. True improvement in life comes from taking action. Actions stem from thoughts, and wise thoughts can develop from reading. Hence, some reading is necessary—but only to a point. That's sufficient.

More specifically, reading to understand capitalism is essential. It's a game, and learning the strategies is vital. No additional knowledge is typically necessary for ordinary labor, but learning about asset acquisition, holding, and disposal is crucial. Capitalism is what it is because the capitalists are ruthless.

From there, relentless action must follow. While you may need to read occasionally to fill gaps in your knowledge, all your energy must be focused on action.

Creating something from nothing doesn't require maximum intelligence; it requires maximum horsepower. Ultimately, whether successful or not, the goal is to produce significant results, and that's where the focus should be.

If a process is difficult or exhausting but yields few results in a short period, overall "horsepower" is lacking. Low horsepower leads to defeat in competition.

Exercise

I strongly recommend exercise; it's not just necessary, it's transformative. Though boosting health and aesthetics are significant benefits, they are not the primary reasons to hit the gym.

The main purpose of regular exercise is to ensure you don't implode during the long journey ahead—to put it bluntly, to keep from going insane. It's a vital strategy to maintain sanity through the harsh years of striving for wealth. Exercise is one of the most cost-effective ways to manage stress.

Learning philosophy through physical exertion also has great advantages. Exposing yourself to the limits of physical pain repeatedly can significantly boost your mental resilience. Reflecting on it, intense physical activity seems to enhance stress tolerance; when your body endures severe pain, mental suffering momentarily fades. This robust stress tolerance is a critical ingredient for achieving maximum performance, driving relentless action forward.

Those familiar with marathons will understand the philosophy of a different kind of workout. There's a phenomenon known as "Second Wind."

This term describes the state during intense exercise when, somewhat counterintuitively, pain decreases and breathing becomes more regular. As blood flow improves, the body adapts from the initial respiratory distress and chest pain to a more manageable condition, often referred to as a secondary steady state.

For instance, the toughest part of a 10-mile run is typically the first mile. It's hard to regulate your breathing, and you might feel pain in your lungs and airways. However, once you surpass that initial mile, your respiratory system adjusts to the demands of the activity, making it easier to maintain a regular breathing filter. This makes the remaining distance much more manageable.

Exercise is a part of work, and work is a part of exercise. Whether it's for a regular paycheck or not, every struggle to maximize your income or to build an income system is essentially a form of work. These efforts are most challenging at the start, but as time goes on and both body and spirit find their rhythm, moving forward becomes easier. Exercise teaches you this philosophy in a very direct, physical way.

Relationships

It's best to minimize relationships, and if you are genuinely committed, they will naturally diminish. Understanding and facing the world's factual reality logically transforms one from a popular figure to an outlier. While crowds may seem normal, upon closer inspection, they are not.

What does "normal" mean? In its simplest definition, it refers to existing circumstances. Living in a capitalist system of any advanced country, truly facing capitalism means striving to become a capitalist, as it's the standard strategy to succeed in this system. This is considered "normal" in our contemporary society.

Achieving this is not primarily about difficulty; no one else will care or take this journey for you. Imagine how few are truly building an empire from zero to over $10 million in assets without excuses or hesitation.

When individuals with opposing thoughts and philosophies meet, conflicts naturally arise, or if one is wise, they simply distance themselves. Once you truly commit to this path, you become a minority, often estranged from the majority.

Statistically, in South Korea, only about 0.84% of the population own net cash assets over $1 million. That's roughly one in a hundred people. Reflect on how rare that is.

Thus, solitude becomes your shadow.

Yet, there are a few with a resolve similar to yours. Throughout life, you will encounter some of these individuals. It's essential to form alliances and unite with them. The world is a formidable opponent, and when possible, it's logical to join forces.

For instance, living together under one roof with such people can reduce living costs and naturally allows sharing of strengths and resources, which can also diminish the sense of loneliness. Moreover, observing each other's progress spurs internal competition, enhancing individual resolve and strength.

Having siblings offers an optimal setup under these circumstances. Building a strong empire under a shared ideology with blood-related siblings forms an elite squad, arguably the most reliable alliance one could have. I am grateful to have such siblings; our coalition is progressing with clear and concrete visions for the next five and ten years. Together, we share these beliefs and engage daily in honorable endeavors.

EPILOGUE

Do not pity yourself. Do not see yourself as unfortunate. Do not declare life to be devoid of luck or good fortune, for a simple reason: it's not true.

Regardless of your situation, you were born a citizen of one of the world's top economies, reading this in your native language. You could have been born in North Korea, in a war-torn third-world country, or in current hot zones like Russia or Ukraine, forced into a battlefield.

I have consistently made the best moves possible given my circumstances. Over the past 12 years, I have worked in risky, dirty, and morally challenging environments to earn money quickly, repeatedly facing life-threatening situations. Now, I am striving to reach the upper echelons, continuously pushing myself to the limit. I will be reborn as the best version of myself.

Some households endure due to physical or mental illness,

others crumble due to unfortunate incidents, and some suffer through poor relationships.

I truly do not believe I was born under an unlucky star. I don't think so because it's not true and because it's not the best strategic move I can make in my situation.

In every family, there tends to be at least one individual who bravely confronts adverse situations. These are the future leaders, the heroes.

What is a hero? Think of Batman, Iron Man, Captain America, Superman. They share courage and strength, enduring prolonged periods of great pain and solitude. Becoming the hero of a struggling family lineage, enduring pain, isn't necessarily bad; in fact, it's a positive sign. It's a signal that you are indeed a hero.

Our heroes live daily in intense pain and solitude, but this should be embraced defiantly. When I feel pain and solitude, I smile because I realize I am growing stronger. No matter how severe the pain or solitude, the fact that I stand firm, breathe, earn money, do push-ups, and run shows that I am stronger than any negative emotion.

Laugh at those negative feelings. Rebel against them. Live defiantly, as Albert Camus suggested.
Even if the gods are against you, they will not be able to stop you.
We are not now that strength which in old days
Moved earth and heaven, that which we are, we are;
One equal temper of heroic hearts,
Made weak by time and fate, but strong in will
To strive, to seek, to find, and not to yield.

As quoted from Alfred Lord Tennyson's poem "Ulysses" in the movie "007 SKYFALL".

www.ingramcontent.com/pod-product-compliance
Lightning Source LLC
Chambersburg PA
CBHW071956210526
45479CB00003B/956